On the Go
planes

KU-238-245

David and Penny Glover

BROMLEY LIBRARIES

3 0128 70093 2315

First published in 2007 by Wayland

Copyright © Wayland 2007

This paperback edition published in 2011 by Wayland

Wayland
338 Euston Road
London NW1 3BH

Wayland
Level 17/207 Kent Street
Sydney, NSW 2000

All rights reserved.

Editor: Camilla Lloyd
Editorial Assistant: Katie Powell
Designer: Elaine Wilkinson
Picture Researcher: Kathy Lockley

Picture Acknowledgements: The author and publisher would like to thank the following for allowing these pictures to be reproduced in this publication: Cover: Airbus (main), Mark Wagner/aviation-images.com; Airbus, S.A.S. 2006: 2, 4, 8, 10, 12, 19; Scott Tucker/Alamy: 6, Michael Dwyer/Alamy: 7, Roger Bamber/Alamy: 13, Mark Hamilton/Alamy: 16b, Transtock Inc./Alamy: 21; Reuters/Corbis: 1, 14, 20, James Leynse/Corbis: 9, Peter Blakely/Corbis: 11, David Lawrence/Corbis: 18; Mark Wagner/ aviation-images.com: 16t; Science Museum: 22; Jochen Tack/Still Pictures: 5, Christopher Papsch/Still Pictures: 15; VirginAtlanticGlobalFlyer: 17.

With special thanks to Airbus, S.A.S. 2006.

British Library Cataloguing in Publication Data
Glover, David, 1953 Sept. 4-
    Planes. - (On the go)
    1. Airplanes - Juvenile literature
    I. Title II. Glover, Penny
    629.1'33

ISBN-13: 978 0 7502 6699 4

Printed in China

Wayland is a division of Hachette Children's Book

Contents

What are planes?

Planes are vehicles that can fly. They have **wings** and they fly through the air.

wings

Planes fly high in the sky. They carry passengers to different places.

rotor

Helicopters have **rotors** instead of wings. The rotor spins in the air to make them fly. This police helicopter is hovering above the ground watching the traffic.

Plane quiz
What does a helicopter have instead of wings?

Plane parts

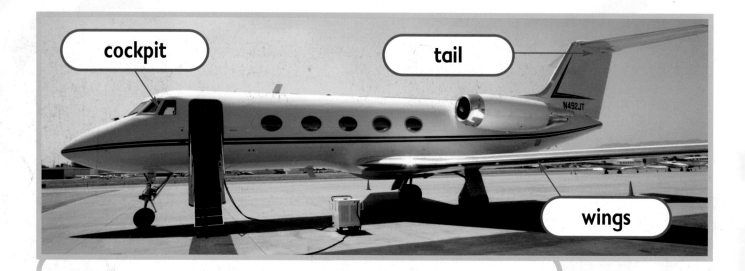

cockpit

tail

wings

The **pilot** sits in the **cockpit** and flies the plane. When the plane is on the ground it stands on legs with wheels The **tail** helps the plane fly straight.

Plane quiz
Where does the pilot sit?

The helicopter pilot sits in the cockpit underneath the rotor.

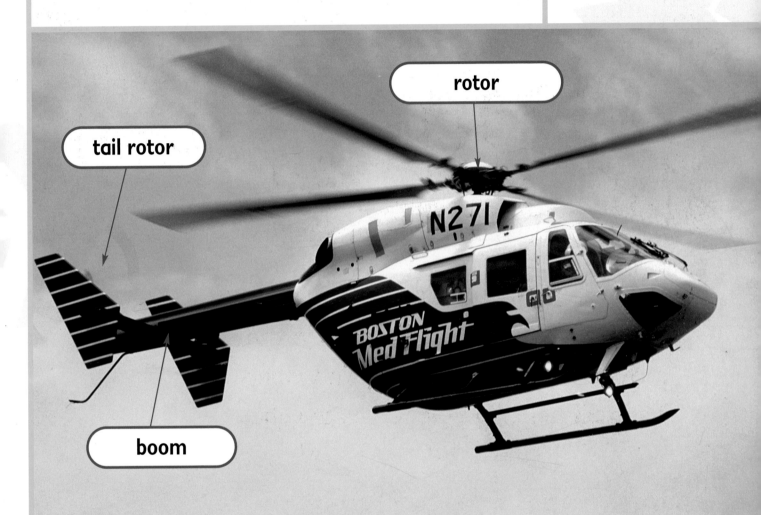

rotor

tail rotor

boom

The **boom** and tail rotor stop the helicopter from spinning around when it is in the air.

What is inside?

The pilot sits at the **flight deck** inside the cockpit.

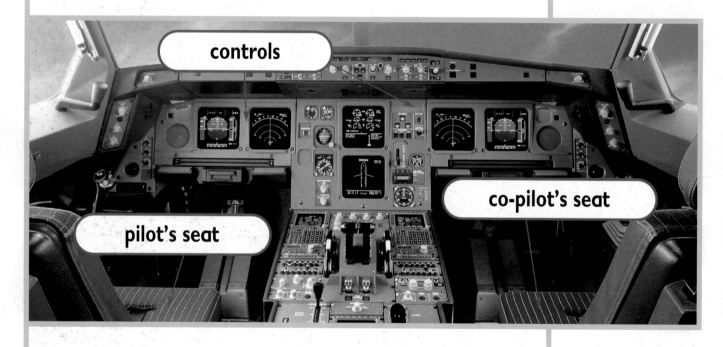

controls

co-pilot's seat

pilot's seat

The pilot is surrounded by controls, switches, dials and computer screens. The co-pilot helps the pilot fly the plane.

Inside a passenger plane the passengers sit in comfortable seats. There are sometimes televisions to watch to pass the time.

Plane quiz

Who helps the pilot fly the plane?

How do they fly?

Some planes have powerful **jet engines** that push them through the air.

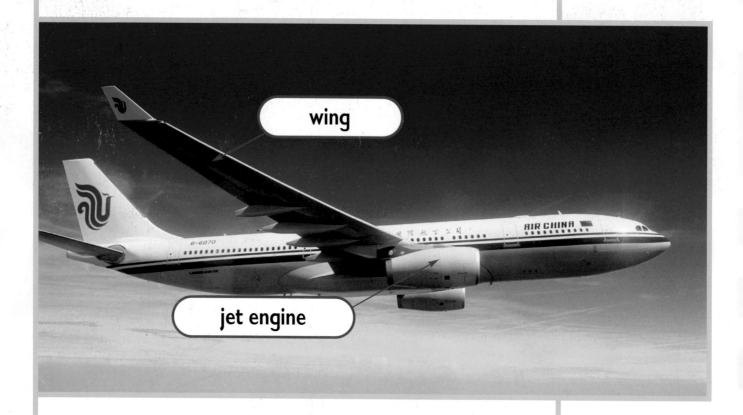

wing

jet engine

The plane's wings are curved on top. Their special shape makes the plane fly.

tanker

At the airport a tanker fills the **fuel** tanks. The fuel tanks are inside the wings.

Plane quiz

Where are the fuel tanks on a plane?

Take off and landing

runway

The plane takes off from a long **runway** at an airport. The plane speeds down the runway on its wheels. When it is going fast enough, it lifts off the ground.

The runway must be clear when the plane lands. At night runway lights mark the path the plane must follow.

runway lights

Plane quiz
Where does an aeroplane take off?

Planes to the rescue!

winch

wire

harness

These people are being rescued from a flood by a helicopter. The helicopter lifts them to safety. They sit in a **harness** at the end of the wire. Then the **winch** winds them up.

A **transport plane** can drop food to places where there are starving people. Parachutes carry the boxes safely to the ground.

Plane quiz

How does a helicopter rescue people?

Record breakers

The biggest plane

The Antonov 225 is the biggest plane in the world. It is so big it can carry a space shuttle on its back.

The fastest jet

The SR-71 Blackbird is the fastest jet in the world. It can fly at more than two thousand miles per hour.

Global Flyer

The first plane to fly non-stop around the world without refuelling was called the Global Flyer. It took three days.

Plane quiz

How fast can the SR-71 Blackbird fly?

Flying safely

Planes go very fast, but flying is a safe way to travel. **Air traffic controllers** tell pilots when to land and take off. They make sure that the planes do not crash.

Inside the plane passengers fasten their **seat belts** for take off and landing. The **cabin** crew tell the passengers what to do in an emergency.

Plane quiz

When should passengers always fasten their seatbelts?

Special planes

Some planes take part in amazing displays. The Red Arrows display team fly close together. This is called **flying in formation**.

coloured smoke

A **biplane** has two wings, one above the other. Biplanes are good for **stunt** flying because they can spin and turn quickly. Sometimes a person stands on the top wing while the plane is flying.

Plane quiz
Why are biplanes good for stunt flying?

Old Planes

The Flyer was the first aeroplane to fly. It was built by the Wright brothers, over one hundred years ago. With one person on board, its first flight lasted just 12 seconds.

Plane words

air traffic controller
Someone who tells pilots when to take off and land. They make sure the planes at the airport do not crash into each other.

biplane
A plane with two wings, one above the other.

boom
A helicopter's tail. The tail rotor is at the end of the boom.

cabin
The place where the passengers sit.

cockpit
The place where the pilot sits.

flight deck
The inside of the cockpit where the pilot flies the plane.

flying in formation
When several planes fly together in a pattern.

harness
The straps that fasten someone to the wire so that the helicopter can lift them from the ground.

jet engine
An engine that pushes a plane through the air.

fuel
Something that burns inside an engine to make it work.

pilot
The person who flies a plane.

rotor
The blades that spin to make a helicopter fly.

runway
The long, flat strip where planes take off and land.

seat belt
A safety strap that holds passengers in their seats.

stunt
Trick such as a loop or a spin performed by a special plane.

tail
The back part of a plane that helps it to fly straight and to steer.

transport plane
A plane that carries loads such as mail or emergency supplies.

winch
A drum that winds up a wire rope like the one on a rescue helicopter.

wing
The large surfaces that make a plane fly as it travels through the air.

Quiz answers

Page 5 Rotors.

Page 6 In the cockpit.

Page 9 The co-pilot.

Page 11 In the wings.

Page 13 From a runway.

Page 15 It lifts them to safety with a winch, wire and harness.

Page 17 At more than two thousand miles an hour.

Page 19 For take off and landing.

Page 21 They can spin and turn quickly.

Index